TRACING
YOUR
FAMILY HIST~~~~

MERCHANT
NAVY

compiled by Allison E Duffield
edited by Sarah Paterson

IMPERIAL WAR MUSEUM

IMPERIAL WAR

MUSEUM

ISBN 1 904 89727 4
2nd Edition
© Trustees of the Imperial War Museum, 2005

CONTENTS

PREFACE

Day in, day out – and for many years past – rather more than a third of all the public enquiries received by the Museum's Department of Printed Books staff have concerned family history. In many cases we answer these using our knowledge of military history and military institutions and with information from our own rich collections. However, we can also provide accurate referral to the many sources and contacts we know, both elsewhere in the Museum and at scores of other specialist institutions and resources far and wide. The details change over time and new sources emerge. We have to keep up to date with these developments if we are to maintain the quality of our service. With the *Tracing Your Family History* series we aim to share our knowledge with you, helping you to find and understand the information that is available. This second edition of *Tracing Your Family History: Merchant Navy* does just that. It has been comprehensively revised with all the latest information that we ourselves use in our enquiry work.

We are grateful for all the advice and help we have received from Museum colleagues and from other organisations in the preparation of this guide and its predecessor.

Richard Golland
Keeper
Department of Printed Books

ABOUT THE MUSEUM

One of the founding principles behind the establishment of the Imperial War Museum (IWM) in 1917 was its function as a collective memory. Although the original plan for listing the names of the fallen as an intrinsic part of the building never materialised, the Museum has always regarded the individual and his or her experience as being of paramount importance. In his opening address in June 1920, Sir Alfred Mond 'the father of the Imperial War Museum' declared the hope that the collection would be made *'so complete that every individual, man or woman, sailor, soldier, airman or civilian who contributed, however obscurely, to the final result, may be able to find in these galleries an example or illustration of the sacrifice he made or the work he did, and in the archives some record of it.'* Consequently, today the Museum can offer a wealth of material to the family history researcher.

A walk around the main displays on the major conflicts of the century at the Museum in Lambeth Road can help provide a context for a relative's service. There are also additional branches at Duxford in Cambridgeshire, HMS *Belfast*, moored on the Thames opposite the Tower of London, the Churchill Museum and Cabinet War Rooms off Whitehall and Imperial War Museum North in Manchester.

The scope of the Museum encompasses all twentieth century conflict, concentrating on the British and Commonwealth involvement since 1914. In an age of total war, every family in the United Kingdom has been affected in some way. The study of family history, perhaps boosted by the greater availability of information on the internet, has grown considerably over recent years. From schoolchildren interviewing grandparents, to local historians writing commemorative histories, the burgeoning growth of this popular activity has made it a real industry. Many of the individuals engaged in research can learn much from the material housed at the Imperial War Museum – original art works and objects of war, personal letters and diaries, contemporary film and photographs, retrospective recorded interviews, and the invaluable collection of printed materials, journals, maps and ephemera. Research may be done in any of the reference departments of the Museum – the Departments of Art, Documents, Exhibits and Firearms, Film and Photograph Archives, Printed Books and the Sound Archive. Access to these collections is both welcomed and encouraged, although a prior appointment is usually necessary. Initial approaches can be made by telephone, letter or email, and staff can provide advice about how to proceed with an enquiry and what materials might be available.

For the family researcher, the first port of call will generally be the Department of Printed Books. This constitutes a national reference library containing well over 150,000 books and pamphlets, 30,000 journals and an impressive range of individual maps and ephemera items, such as ration-books, propaganda leaflets and song-sheets. It is important to stress that the Imperial War Museum **does not** hold any personal service records or official documentation, although through both this booklet and our normal enquiry service, we can offer advice on what and where remaining sources may still be found. We do have a wide range of items in our collections which will assist the researcher. These can all be consulted under one roof, with experienced staff on-hand to direct and answer enquiries.

The primary aim of this booklet is to help the enquirer find out about individuals who served in the Merchant Navy. Some basic information is given in the following paragraphs and useful book titles, which will help those unfamiliar with the subject, are given in the bibliography at the end. All of these titles are held by the Museum and can be consulted in the Reading Room, but for those unable to make a personal visit, full publication details are given to enable other copies of the books to be ordered through the public library system. Addresses of the various institutions, which may assist, can also be found listed in Appendix II.

Detailed information about merchant seamen who have been taken captive will not be found in here, nor will you find advice on sources for the Commonwealth forces. If you do have any queries on either of these subjects please consult us for separate guidance.

Strenuous efforts have been made to ensure that the information contained in this booklet is accurate. If any errors have inadvertently been made, we would appreciate it if these could be drawn to our attention so that amendments can appear in later editions.

ORGANISATION OF THE MERCHANT NAVY

The sea, shipping and seamen have always been extremely important to an island nation. There has always been a close connection between the Merchant Navy and the Royal Navy (which can cause some confusion for the family historian). The primary functions of the Merchant Navy are trade and transport, whilst the Royal Navy's vessels are armed for a defence role. Since 1864 merchant vessels have been distinguished by the Red Ensign (red flag with the Union Jack in the top corner next to the flagstaff), often affectionately known as the 'Red Duster'. Some sailors served in both fleets, and especially during times of war, the Merchant Navy has expanded to play a crucial role, with many of its men becoming part of the Royal Naval Reserve and some of its ships being requisitioned by the Royal Navy. During the twentieth century the Merchant Navy Fleet has declined in size, although it is still possible for shipping to be requisitioned by the Ministry of Defence. The last time this happened in a sizable way was in the Falklands Conflict of 1982.

The term *Merchant Navy* is used throughout this book, although it only came into use in 1922 when it was bestowed by King George V to demonstrate a nation's thanks for their enormous efforts in the First World War. Before that date it was variously known as the *Merchant Service*, the *Mercantile Marine* or the *Merchant Marine*. In 1918 a uniform was adopted, but this was not compulsory and different shipping companies were allowed to retain some elements of their own distinctive house design, such as buttons or cap badge. Unlike the Armed Forces, the

Merchant Navy was not a single entity – it was a loose formation of a large number of different shipping companies conducting trade and business, many of which were in competition with each other. It was essentially a civilian service, with men serving aboard a ship for the duration of the voyage. During both world wars enormous courage was displayed by the men of the 'Fourth Service' who kept the country supplied with food and precious raw materials, despite the perils of the oceans and the menace of vicious submarine warfare.

It is also worth pointing out that although we use the term 'seamen' throughout this book, not all members of the Merchant Navy were male. During both world wars the vast majority of those who served at sea were men, but some women also served (primarily, although not exclusively, in a stewardess role) and the information contained here applies to both sexes.

On the outbreak of the First World War the administration of the Merchant Navy was divided between the Board of Trade and the Admiralty Transport Department. In 1916 the Ministry of Shipping was established. This allowed the government to control and regulate merchant shipping and enabled the war effort to be conducted as efficiently as possible. In 1917 Ministry of Shipping took over control of the Admiralty Transport Department. In the same year, responsibility for shipbuilding, formerly shared between the Admiralty and the Board of Trade, was also taken over. The Ministry of Shipping was dissolved in March 1921 and its responsibilities passed to the Mercantile Marine Department of the Board of Trade.

In October 1939 the Ministry of Shipping was re-established to undertake the functions of the Sea Transport Division, the Mercantile Marine Department of the Board of Trade. Control of shipbuilding was transferred to the Admiralty in February 1940. In May 1941 the Ministry of Shipping and Ministry of Transport merged to form the Ministry of War Transport (divided into the Ship Management Division, Sea Transport Division and the Marine Crews Division). In 1946 the word 'War' was dropped from the title.

SHIPPING

The Merchant Navy consists of many different shipping companies made up of varying numbers and types of vessels. The various types of ship can be divided into four main groupings:

PASSENGER VESSELS

Ships designed to carry people vary in size from luxurious *passenger liners* to *yachts*. *Cross-channel vessels, ferries* and *paddle-steamers* also fall into this category. Many of these served as *troop-carriers* or *hospital ships* during both world wars. Some vessels were converted into *armed merchant cruisers*; these would patrol the trade routes and protect vital incoming consignments of food, equipment and supplies. Paddle-steamers might also be converted into *minesweepers*. The vastly increased threat of aerial attack in the Second World War meant that many vessels were fitted out to provide anti-aircraft protection. During the Second World War some paddle-steamers saw service as *anti-aircraft escorts* for convoys and coastal patrols. Also in the Second World War, some passenger (and cargo) liners were used as *infantry assault ships* or *landing craft* (although many of these were purpose built).

CARGO VESSELS

Cargo ships primarily carry goods for trade, rather than passengers (although many vessels have the necessary facilities to carry a few paying passengers as well). The *cargo liner* will be a large fast vessel – the term 'liner' relates to a ship that sails to a regular timetable between scheduled ports (usually just the outward and destination port). In contrast, the *tramp* (sometimes known as the *universal carrier*) can be chartered to serve anywhere in the world, whenever it is needed. Some cargo vessels carry a specific type of commodity, such as *oil tankers* or *ore carriers*. *Colliers* (carrying coal) and *coasters* (carrying freight) are more domestic vessels and ply their trade around the British coastline, and some European ports. During both wars they performed sterling work in bringing supplies into the country. In the First World War some acted as *Q-ships* – these were ships that looked just like normal cargo vessels but had in fact been fitted with hidden arms so that the enemy could be engaged at close range.

FISHING VESSELS

Trawlers and *Drifters* are the two main types of fishing vessel. Trawlers are the larger of the two. They catch fish by trawling (or towing) a long conical shaped net through which the fish enters and cannot escape. The Drifters are smaller and would seldom journey far from their home port. The fish are caught in the nets which form a vertical wall in which they are trapped. During both world wars the vessels were primarily used for patrolling and for minesweeping.

AUXILIARY AND SUPPORT VESSELS

This covers an enormous variety of vessels, of which the *tug* is one of the most important. Primarily based in home waters (although there were also larger ocean-going tugs) she often played many different roles, such as patrolling, intercepting, assisting river barges, helping ships into berths and salvage. Other vessels include *dredgers*, which ensure the entrances to harbours and ports are clear of mud, rock and sand, and *cable-layers*.

OFFICERS

Most officers receive the title of *Master* or *Mate* either as a result of examination or years of experience.

Bearing in mind the extremely wide variety of types of vessel, you can understand how it is very difficult to make generalisations about the crew that would be carried. What follows is an attempt to describe the officers working for a large shipping company specialising in passenger liners.

Commodore is the title given to the most senior Master in a shipping company. He will usually command the newest and largest vessel in the fleet, also known as the 'flagship'. The senior person on board most ships is the *Captain* (he may also be known as the *Master* or *Commander*). He is responsible for the safety of the ship and any passengers carried, as well as the efficiency of the officers and crew. *Skipper* is another title used, usually on smaller vessels, especially those of the Fishing Fleets. The *Chief Officer*, or *First Mate*, is the 'second-in-command.' He is responsible for the smooth running and navigation of the vessel and is also usually responsible for any cargo carried. Beneath him will be the *Second, Third* or *Fourth Officers* (or *Mates*). In addition, many larger vessels carry junior officers as *Cadets, Midshipmen* or *Apprentices*, as part of their on board training.

The *Chief Engineer* is responsible for all the Engine Room Staff and reports directly to the Master. Next in line is the *Assistant Chief Engineer*, followed by the *Second, Third* and *Fourth Engineers*.

Depending on the size of the vessel and the number of passengers carried, *Surgeons, Medical Officers* or *Nursing Sisters* may also be carried on board. *Wireless Officers* and *Signal Officers* are also employed, as is a *Purser* (often assisted by *Assistant* or *Deputy Pursers*) who looks after clerical, financial, victualling and welfare matters.

The situation would change in times of war and the complement and their duties changed radically as many merchant vessels were requisitioned and converted for war work. In the case of larger vessels, a regular naval Captain was appointed to command the vessel. The original Captain/Master, if not already in the Royal Navy Reserves, was given a temporary commission as a Commander and retained to advise the naval Captain. Gunnery officers, Signal officers and a number of naval ratings were also appointed for general duties. Nearly all the ship's engineers were normally retained as they were used to the workings of their vessel's engines. Merchant Navy officers were often given temporary commissions, equal to their 'rank' in peacetime. In many cases the crew were already in the Royal Fleet Reserve or Royal Naval Reserve and so adapted well to the change. However, few were signals experts, so men from the Royal Naval Volunteer Reserve usually took over these duties.

CREW

The *Boatswain* is the 'buffer' between the officers and the men and is the most senior rating in charge of the crew. The *Carpenter* also has his own staff and is responsible for any repairs to the vessel's equipment, including the all-important steering gear. The *Quartermaster* will have had a great deal of experience at sea; they undertake many duties including taking a turn at the wheel. *Able-Bodied Seamen* (sometimes called *Leading Seamen*) are qualified sailors, who have been promoted from *Ordinary Seamen*. *Boys* are seamen in training.

The Engine Room Staff is made up of specialists according to the size and type of the vessel and its cargo. The *Donkeyman* is the most senior engine room rating. In addition, larger vessels may carry *Greasers*, who are experienced Firemen; these help ensure the smooth running of the machinery and are responsible for the work of the *Firemen* (who had to keep the fires burning beneath the boilers) and the *Trimmers* (who ensured the supply of coal). Their work was more important in coal fuelled vessels and the numbers declined in oil fuelled vessels.

The *Purser's* Department is very important, especially in large passenger ships. The Purser is assisted by the *Chief Steward* (who sometimes ranks as an officer), and is in turn assisted by the *Deputy* (or *Assistant*) *Stewards*. The Steward's Department is made up of *Cooks, Butchers* and *Bakers* in the galleys and *Waiters* for duties in the dining rooms, cabins and decks.

During wartime when vessels were requisitioned or converted for war service, the crew situation might change. Smaller vessels, like coastal craft and trawlers, were also requisitioned for a vast range of wartime duties. Generally, the complement remained the same, with the addition of naval Petty Officers for signals duties. The Skipper was given a warrant rank in the Royal Naval Reserve. Some of the crew might have already been in the Reserves and therefore would have had some training in the use of gunnery. After the periods of war ended merchant seamen would resume their more normal duties.

SERVICE RECORDS

There are a variety of sources that will provide information about those who served in the Merchant Navy. As has been previously stated, the Imperial War Museum has no official unpublished documentation relating to service. However, detailed below are a number of archives, which may be of assistance. Please note that some will only release information to the individual concerned, the next of kin or legal beneficiary, although some may release details to other interested parties who have prior consent from the individual concerned or their next of kin. In most cases search fees will be levied. Enquirers are recommended to put their requests in writing, quoting in full, the name and as much factual information as is already known on the service of the individual concerned. If no details are known, some basic information may be available from the *Absent Voters Lists* of 1918 and the *Service Voters Registers* of 1945, compiled in order to enable seamen to vote in the constituency of their home address. These should be held by the relevant local library, town hall or county record office.

Most Merchant Navy personnel records are now held by **The National Archives, Ruskin Avenue, Kew, Richmond, Surrey TW9 4DU**. The National Archives was formerly known as the Public Record Office (PRO). The National Archives will conduct research for you (the current rate for this is £15 for 15 minutes), or you can employ a professional researcher (details are available direct from Readers' Services at The National Archives). You can also visit The National Archives yourself – they have produced some very helpful books as well as an excellent series of Records Research Guides that can be accessed directly on their website at

www.nationalarchives.gov.uk Some records are actually available online (for which there is a charge), and the Merchant Navy Second World War Medal Index can be viewed at **www.nationalarchives.gov.uk/documentsonline/seame ns-medals.asp** Books which are especially recommended are: *Tracing Your Ancestors in the Public Record Office*, 6th revised edition edited by Amanda Bevan (Richmond, Surrey: Public Record Office, 2002) and *Records of Merchant Shipping and Seamen* by Kelvin Smith, Christopher T and Michael J Watts (Richmond, Surrey: Public Record Office, 1998). Another useful title by Christopher T and Michael J Watts is *My Ancestor was a Merchant Seaman* (London: Society of Genealogists Enterprises, 2004).

The **Registry of Shipping and Seamen, MCA Cardiff, Ground Floor, Anchor Court, Keen Road, Cardiff CF24 5JW** now holds only current Merchant Navy records. Most of their records from the twentieth century (and earlier) have now been passed to The National Archives.

Another potential source is the **Family Records Centre, 1 Myddelton Street, London EC1R 1UW**, which provides research facilities previously provided at St Catherine's House. Their records include indexes of births, deaths and marriages since 1837, legal adoptions since 1927; and births, deaths and marriages of some British citizens abroad since the late eighteenth century. There are current plans to relocate the Family Records Centre to The National Archives in 2008.

In addition, there are many records relating to genealogical research available for public consultation at the **Guildhall Library, Lloyd's Marine Collection, Aldermanbury,**

London EC2P 2EJ, the **National Maritime Museum, Romney Road, Greenwich, London SE10 9NF, Merseyside Maritime Museum, Archives and Library, Albert Dock, Liverpool L3 4AQ** and the **Southampton Archives, Southampton City Council, South Block, Civic Centre, Southampton SO14 7LY**. This is not an exhaustive list of institutions, and you should remember that appointments to view these collections (and others mentioned in Appendix II) must be made in advance of arrival.

RECORDS OF OFFICERS

MASTER AND MATES

In 1845 a Register of Masters began to be compiled. In that year the first examinations for Masters and Mates were introduced (initially on a voluntary basis, but these became compulsory from 1850). Success in these formal Board of Trade examinations resulted in a Certificate of Competency. Certificates of Service were also given to those who had many years of experience at sea.

The National Archives holds the Registers of Certificates for Masters and Mates in the series of Registers at *BT 122-BT 128*, covering the years 1845-1925. The different Registers cover Foreign and Home Trade, as well as Colonial, and are arranged in Certificate number order. Details include name, place and date of birth, full name, rank examined for or served in, and place of issue and date of certificate. *BT 127* is a consolidated index.

Also held at The National Archives are:

BT 317 – Registers and Statistics of Passes and Renewals of Certificates of Competency of Masters and Mates, 1913-1977

BT 318 – Registers of Passes and Failures in Examination for Certificates of Masters, Mates and Engineers, 1929-1984

From 1910 a Combined Index to Masters and Mates as well as Engineers and Skippers and Mates of Fishing Boats began. This is available on microfiche for the years 1910-1969 in *BT 352*.

The **National Maritime Museum** holds many of the successful Applications for the Certificates from 1845 to 1927. These may contain additional information, and you should contact the Research Enquiries Section if you are interested in seeing these or having copies made (for which a charge will be levied). The Certificates are arranged in number order, so it is necessary to know this in order to proceed. This can be obtained either through The National Archives sources outlined above or from *Lloyd's Captains' Registers*.

Lloyd's Captains' Registers were produced from 1869-1947 (although entries go back to Masters from 1851 who were still serving in 1869). Entries were based on details supplied to Lloyds by the Registrar General of Shipping and Seamen, and include name, place and date of birth, Certificate number, and date and place of examination as well as a potted history of his service. These can be found at the **Guildhall Library**, but The National Archives has an incomplete set on microfilm. The National Maritime Museum also has a set on microfilm (the quality of which is variable).

ENGINEERS

The system of certification was extended to Engineers in 1862. Certificates of Competency and Service issued to Engineers can be found at The National Archives under the following classes:

BT 139 – Registers of Certificates of Competency, Engineers, 1861-1921

BT 140 – Registers of Certificates of Service, Engineers, Colonial, 1870-1921

BT 142 – Registers of Certificates of Service, Engineers, 1862-1921

An index to the above registers can be found in *BT 141*.

From 1910 to 1969 Engineers can be found under the Combined Index to Certificates of Competency, Masters, Mates, Engineers and Fishing Officers, Home and Foreign Trade, in *BT 352*.

Some information may also be found in:

BT 318 – Registers of Passes and Failures in Examination for Certificates of Masters, Mates and Engineers, 1929-1984

BT 320 – Registers of Passes and Renewals of Engineers' Certificates, 1913-1935

FISHING OFFICERS

In 1884 Certification was introduced for Skippers and Mates (or Second Hands) of fishing vessels. The National Archives holds the following record classes:

BT 129 – Registers of Certificates of Competency, Skippers and Mates of Fishing Boats, 1880-1921

BT 130 – Registers of Certificates of Service, Skippers and Mates of Fishing Boats, 1883-1919

From 1910 to 1969 officers of Fishing Boats can be found under the Combined Index to Certificates of Competency, Masters, Mates, Engineers and Fishing Officers, Home and Foreign Trade, in *BT 352*.

Another possible source to check is *BT 396*, the Registers of Passes and Renewals of Certificates of Competency for Fishing Officers, 1883-1959.

REGISTERS OF SEAMEN'S SERVICE

In general, *Registers of Seamen* are to be found at **The National Archives** in the Board of Trade files. Registration was introduced in 1835, in order for the Admiralty to have an accurate listing of seamen who could be called up in the event of war. The Registers do not run consecutively – for example, there is a gap between 1857 and 1913. Records from 1973 are held by the Registry of Shipping and Seamen, but it is important to be aware that these are application forms for discharge books, and although they will provide some personal details there will not be any information about which ships an individual served on.

What was known as the *Fourth Register* began in October 1913 and continued through to 1941. Unfortunately, large numbers of records between 1913 and 1920 were destroyed which means you may have a problem finding those who served in the First World War (although there are alternative sources that can be used, such as the Crew Lists and Agreements). The following can be viewed on microfiche:

BT 350 - Register of Seamen, Special Index, Alphabetical Series (CR 10 cards) covering the years 1918-1921. These are quite detailed, containing details such as date and place of birth, physical description, rating, discharge number, next of kin, often with a photograph and a list of the ships served on.

BT 349 – Register of Seamen, Central Index, Alphabetical Series, 1921-1941 (CR 1 cards). These are slightly less detailed than those above, but do sometimes contain a photograph.

BT 348 – Register of Seamen, Central Index, Numerical Series, 1921-1941 (CR 2 cards). Unlike the above, which are arranged in order of surname, these are arranged by discharge number. The reverse of the card should contain a listing of the ships (by official number) and the dates the seaman signed on.

BT 364 – Register of Seamen, Combined Index, 1918-1941. This consists of cards extracted from the three indexes listed above, and most relate to men who continued their service after 1941.

The original cards are held by the **Southampton Archives**.

You may also find material in the series of *Seamen's Pouches* in *BT 372* and *BT 390*. Each pouch relates to an individual seaman and consists of an envelope with varying contents. These can include personal documents, such as identity cards, letters and photographs. Unfortunately, it is not a totally comprehensive collection, and although there is coverage for the years between 1913 and 2002, you are more likely to find material for those who served in the 1930s or later.

The Fifth Register, covering the dates between 1941 and 1972, can be found in *BT 382*. This new Registration sequence was introduced when the Essential Work (Merchant Navy) Order was passed in 1941 as a way of ensuring sufficient manpower. Seamen were registered and paid to be part of the Merchant Navy Reserve Pool when they were ashore. For the first time, merchant seamen enjoyed continuous paid employment at sea and on land, whilst the government had a fully detailed and comprehensive register. The Merchant Navy Reserve Pool ceased to exist at the end of March 1947 (when the Merchant Navy Established Service Scheme was set up).

RECORDS OF COOKS

The registration of Cooks began in 1908. Certificates of Competency were granted to those who passed examinations, while Certificates of Service were given to those who qualified as a result of long service. Indexes to the Registers of Cooks' Certificates of Competency and Service, 1913-1956 are held at The National Archives in *BT 319*. The actual Registers covering the period between 1915 and 1958 are held at the **National Maritime Museum**.

CREW LISTS AND AGREEMENTS

A great deal of legislation aimed at improving the lot of the Merchant Seaman was passed in the mid nineteenth century, and one of the most significant benefits was the introduction of the *Articles of Agreements*. These had to provide details of the length, purpose and destination of voyage as well as details of the occupation under which each seaman had been engaged together with his rates of pay. Each member would sign his name (or make his mark next to it) and the whole crew would be 'Signed on Articles' by a Shipping Master in the port from which the ship was sailing. There would be at least two copies of the Agreement (also officially known as T124); one in black print, which would be retained on board the ship, while the red print copy would be sent to the Registrar General of Shipping and Seamen as a record, and would be important in case of any disaster befalling the ship.

Unfortunately, the situation regarding the whereabouts of Crew Agreements is extremely complicated. For the period of the Second World War (and up to 1950) all surviving Agreements and Crew Lists are held by **The National Archives**:

BT 99 – Agreements and Crew Lists, Series II, 1861-1994

BT 100 – Agreements and Crew Lists, Series III (Celebrated Ships), 1835-1999

BT 385 – Index to WWII Ships' Log Books and Agreements and Crew Lists, 1939-1950

BT 380 – War of 1939 to 1945: Log Books, Agreements and Crew Lists and associated records, 1939-1950

BT 381 – Coast Trade Ships Official Log Books and Agreements and Crew Lists, 1939-1946

BT 387 – WWII Log Books and Agreements and Crew Lists of allied foreign ships, requisitioned or chartered by HMG, 1939-1946

The National Archives has only a random 10% sample for the period 1861-1994 in *BT 99* (although there is a good chance that you will find the documentation for famous vessels). The **National Maritime Museum** also has a sample collection, consisting of years that end in a '5' (although this won't be totally complete because some Agreements may still be held at The National Archives under their 'every tenth box' sampling). If you are looking for Agreements from 1865, 1875, 1885, 1895, 1905, 1915, 1925 or 1935, the National Maritime Museum is probably the best place to start your search.

Local Record Offices also took a sample of Crew Agreements between 1863 and 1913.

The remainder (about 70%) of Agreements for the period 1861-1938 were passed to the **Maritime History Archive, Memorial University, St. John's, Newfoundland, A1C 5S7**. Guides to their holdings can be found at The National Archives, or you can see their catalogue online at **www.mun.ca/mha/online.php**

The situation for the years after 1950 is also rather complex. The National Maritime Museum has coverage for the years 1955, 1965, 1975 and 1985, while The National Archives retains its 10% sample. The remainder up to 1976 are held by the Maritime History Archive.

You should be aware that the information you need to retrieve these records is not the ship's name, but her official number. For more information about this, please see the section on Registration of Shipping.

LOG BOOKS

From 1850 it became obligatory for a merchant vessel to keep an official log. This would be divided into two different sections; the *Tabular Section* would record any births, marriages or deaths or other special event that had taken place on board. Sometimes departure dates and times would be included, but these were not compulsory. The *Narrative Section* would contain more details of events that took place, such as accidents, epidemics or disciplinary matters. Their function was not to provide a diary account of the ship's voyage, and they can therefore be a disappointment to the researcher.

If a log has survived (and large numbers have been disposed of, although if a birth or death or other unusual event was recorded these would probably have been retained), it will probably be with the Crew Agreement. All surviving log books for the First World War can be found at **The National Archives** in record class *BT 165*. Other classes for log books include:

BT 380 – War of 1939 to 1945: Log Books, Agreements and Crew Lists and associated records, 1939-1950

BT 381 – Coast Trade Ships Official Log Books and Agreements and Crew Lists, 1939-1946

BT 387 – WWII Log Books and Agreements and Crew Lists of allied foreign ships, requisitioned or chartered by HMG, 1939-1946

An index can be found at BT 385.

Log books for vessels requisitioned by the Admiralty can be found (listed by name) in ADM 53.

You should be aware that the information you need to retrieve these records is not the ship's name, but her official number. For more information about this, please see the section on Registration of Shipping.

REGISTRATION OF SHIPPING

The 'official number' of a vessel is very important, and is often the key to finding out more about her. The reason that a number was used rather than her name, is that it is more constant; names can change every time a ship changes hands, and this may include being sold abroad. In 1854 the registration of shipping came under the control of the Board of Trade, and it was a legal obligation for an owner of a British vessel to register details such as the official number, name and port, who had built her and when, tonnage, construction details and the name of the owner; all changes of ownership were also to be recorded.

In 1890 the system of keeping all the paperwork relating to the ship together was introduced, and they were filed under the date of the vessel's de-registration. You can work this out by looking through *Lloyd's Register of Shipping* or the *Mercantile Navy List* and seeing when the vessel ceases to appear. The records can be found at **The National Archives** in record class *BT 110*. In 1894 registration was extended to fishing vessels which were to be recorded in a separate register.

Lloyd's Register of Shipping is an annual publication (running from mid-summer) listing vessels including their official number with a brief description, date and place of construction, owner, port of registry, etc. Steamers, motor vessels and sailing vessels were listed separately between 1890 and 1947. In 1922 an extra section for trawlers and fishing vessels was introduced.

Lloyd's Register of Yachts (1877-1980) was a similar publication. No issues were produced between 1940-1946.

The *Mercantile Navy List* (1850-1976) was arranged in a similar way. It was divided into two sections for steamers and sailing vessels; and this was later extended to three when motor vessels were added in 1922.

The **Guildhall Library** and **National Maritime Museum** are the best places to go for these publications, but The National Archives have some, and you may be able to find some other copies in good reference libraries around the country. Unfortunately, the Imperial War Museum Department of Printed Books has only a small selection of *Lloyd's Registers* for the period 1914-1940 and the *Mercantile Navy List* for 1913-1966.

PASSENGER LISTS

From 1890 ships' passenger lists were deposited with the Board of Trade by the various shipping lines although copies, often retained by the line, can sometimes be found within the company archives. The lists for the period 1878-1960 can be found in **The National Archives** Board of Trade files *BT 26* for arrivals in United Kingdom ports and *BT 27* for departures from United Kingdom ports. These files are arranged by the port and date of the arrival/departure. There is no index. However, if the name of the vessel is known, the researcher can refer to the *Registers of Passenger Lists*, 1906-1951 in *BT 32*. No passenger lists are held by the Registry of Shipping and Seamen, the National Maritime Museum or the Guildhall Library.

FISHERMEN AND FISHING VESSELS

From 1884 *Crew Lists and Agreements* for fishing vessels were filed separately. As described previously, **The National Archives** now holds those records covering the Second World War period and in addition about 10% of the records, for the periods up to 1938 and after 1951. These are to be found in the Board of Trade files *BT 144* (1884-1929) and in *BT 99* (after 1929). The remaining records are held by the **Maritime History Archive**.

The certificating of Skippers and Mates began in 1884. The National Archives holds the Registers containing these *Certificates of Competency* in *BT 129* and the Registers containing *Certificates of Service* in *BT 130*, with an index in *BT 138*. However, in 1910 a combined index to *Certificates of*

Competence for Masters, Mates, Engineers and Fishing Officers for Foreign and Home Trade was introduced (*BT 352*).

From 1894 all fishing vessels had to be registered. As previously described, relevant records are to be found at The National Archives in the Board of Trade files *BT 110*. Reference should also be made to the annual volumes of *Lloyd's Register of Shipping* and the *Mercantile Navy List*.

Log Books are also split between The National Archives and the Maritime History Archive. However, please note that although Log Books for merchant vessels requisitioned during the First and Second World Wars are to be found in the Admiralty files *ADM 53*, few Logs have survived after 1939 for vessels smaller than an armed merchant cruiser.

ROYAL NAVAL RESERVE

The Royal Naval Reserve Act was passed in 1859, with the intention of maintaining a Reserve recruited from Merchant Seamen and fishermen, who could be called upon to serve with the Royal Navy if an emergency arose. These men made up the **Royal Naval Reserve**, but the twentieth century saw this Reserve further divided into the Royal Naval Reserve Trawler Section, Royal Naval Volunteer Reserve and Royal Fleet Auxiliaries. For more detailed information on the organisation of the Royal Naval Reserve please refer to *Tracing Your Family History: Royal Navy*.

Records of Royal Naval Reserve officers in service during the First World War are now available in the Admiralty files *ADM*

240 at **The National Archives** and are arranged in order of rank and date of seniority. Details of officers in service until 1950, including the Second World War, are still held by **Navy Search, TNT Archive Services, Tetron Point, William Nadin Way, Swadlincote, Derbyshire DE11 0BB**. For the period after 1950 records have been retained by **Data Protection Cell, Director Naval Career Management, Building 1/152, Victory View, HM Naval Base, Portsmouth, Hampshire PO1 3PX**. Genealogical enquiries to Navy Search and Data Protection Cell should be made in writing and a search fee (currently £30.00) may be levied.

Records of Royal Naval Reserve ratings in service during the period 1914-1958 have also been retained by The National Archives in the Board of Trade files *BT 377*.

An officer's career in the Royal Naval Reserves can also be traced through the editions of the *Navy List*, published continually from 1814. These contain seniority lists, cross-referred to individual ships, which in turn list their complement of officers. During the First and Second World Wars much of the usual information was omitted from the published editions of the *Navy List* and confined to confidential editions for 'service use' only. A full set is held by The National Archives and the **National Maritime Museum**, but the Department of Printed Books holds a near complete run, including many of the confidential editions, for the period 1914 to date.

A selection of records for Merchant Seamen who joined the Royal Naval Reserve are also held by The National Archives in the Board of Trade files *BT 348, BT 349, BT 350* and *BT 364*. The originals of these records have been retained by the

Southampton Archives. Records of the **Merchant Navy Reserve Pool**, for the Second World War, are held at the National Maritime Museum. These lists are arranged alphabetically by name, and include date of birth, their date of acceptance into the Pool as well as the rank and last ship they had served on, and next of kin. Sometimes a photograph is included.

MEDAL RECORDS
AND AWARDS

Awards for service and acts of gallantry were first made to Merchant Seamen in the middle of the nineteenth century. This system was administered by the Marine Department of the Board of Trade. Records of these awards are available for public consultation at **The National Archives** and the **Guildhall Library**.

Campaign medals were awarded for participation in a particular campaign, or for service in time of war. Often a 'clasp' was added to the ribbon of these medals to denote a particular campaign. The 'clasp' was also used to denote second or subsequent awards of Long Service and Good Conduct medals.

First World War campaign medals usually included the name of the recipient, engraved either on the rim, or on the back of the medal. Unfortunately, during the Second World War these medals were not stamped with these details, although arrangements could be made to have this done privately.

For more detailed information on the medals themselves and the range of the awards available, please refer to the publications listed in Appendix III. Those with internet access may also be interested in the Imperial War Museum's website: **www.iwm.org.uk/server/show/ConWebDoc.986** has details on some First World War campaign medals.

Records of campaign medals, awarded during the First World War, including the 1914-15 Star, British War Medal and Victory

Medal, are to be found at The National Archives in the Admiralty files *ADM 171*, for which there are index volumes available. There is a separate group of files for each medal. Records of the Mercantile Marine Medal are available in the Board of Trade files *BT 351*.

Records relating to Second World War campaign medals can now be viewed online at **www.nationalarchives.gov.uk /documentsonline/seamens-medals.asp** You can search the index free of charge, but to view and printout a record the current fee is £3.50. These records can also be consulted at The National Archives, in record class *BT 395*. The medals include the 1939-45 Star, the Africa Star, Atlantic Star, Burma Star, France and Germany Star, Italy Star, Pacific Star and the War Medal. Medals had to be claimed rather than being automatically issued, and if your relative's medals were never issued, the place to contact for proof of entitlement is: **Registry of Shipping and Seamen, MCA Cardiff, Anchor Court, Keen Road, Cardiff CF24 5JW**. You may also need to conduct some research in records now held at The National Archives.

You can find a list of post Second World War campaign medals issued, through the Registry of Shipping and Seamen pages at **www.mcga.gov.uk**

Gallantry medals were awarded for a particular gallant act. The addition of a 'bar' to the medal ribbon of the original medal denotes a second or subsequent award for gallant or distinguished service.

The amount of information available on these awards does vary considerably. Notification of an award would normally be published in the *London Gazette*, sometimes accompanied by the citation (or a short description of why the award was made). However, there was often a considerable delay between the date of the award and the date that the notification and citation were published. It should also be noted that, although individuals may have been recommended for a particular medal, another award might have been substituted. Awards notified in either of the two half-yearly honours lists ('New Year' and 'Birthday') are not normally accompanied by a citation.

For the range of the awards available to personnel of the Merchant Navy please refer to the list of abbreviations in Appendix I. For information on the awards themselves, refer to the publications listed in Appendix III and the Imperial War Museum's website.

In general, gallantry at sea awards for the period 1856-1981 are to be found at The National Archives in the Board of Trade files *BT 261* and the Ministry of Transport files *MT 9* (which include the Albert Medals for saving life at sea for the period 1903-1950). However, records of the Lloyd's Medals for Gallantry at Sea are to be found at the **Guildhall Library**. Although these records include some citations, those not available may be obtained from the **Council Secretariat, Corporation of Lloyd's, 1 Lime Street, London EC3M 7HA**.

Many Merchant Navy seamen received naval gallantry awards during the First and Second World Wars. Records of these are held at The National Archives in Admiralty files *ADM 116* for the First World War and *ADM 1* for the Second World War.

Index volumes are held in *ADM 12*. In addition Merchant Navy fleet rolls of honour, for the First and Second World Wars are to be found in the Board of Trade files *BT 339*.

The medal offices at the Registry of Shipping and Seamen also deal with medal claims and/or replacements. Please note that replacement medals may only be issued to the recipient, or if deceased, to the next of kin. It will also be necessary to provide official documentary proof of entitlement.

A good source of reference for medal awards and medal citations is the *London Gazette*. However, at the beginning of the Second World War, the publication of all citations for gallantry awards was suspended. All enquiries regarding citations for gallantry awards not published in the *London Gazette* should be referred to the **Naval Secretary (Honours and Awards), Room G10, Fleet Headquarters, West Battery, Whale Island, Portsmouth, Hampshire PO2 8DX**.

The Department of Printed Books holds a near complete run of the *London Gazette* from 1914 but, unfortunately, without a complete set of the all important indexes. The National Archives has a full set as does the Guildhall Library, and you may also find copies in some of the larger reference libraries in your area. The *London Gazette* is now also available online and you can check the awards of gallantry medals, promotions of officers or the naturalisation of a relative by using the website **www.gazettes-online.co.uk** The Historic Archive contains First and Second World War issues only (1914-1920 and 1939-1948).

Generally the Department of Printed Books holds published sources only, some of which are listed in Appendix III, but we recommend in particular the volumes of *Seedie's Rolls of Honour and Awards* published by Ripley Registers.

CASUALTY RECORDS

Registers of death at sea are held at **The National Archives** (up to 1964). The **Registry of Shipping and Seamen** still retains the later Registers. Similar records are also held by the **Guildhall Library** and the **National Maritime Museum**.

As we have seen, births, deaths and marriages of passengers and crew at sea were recorded in a Ship's Log. From 1874 these were reported to the Registrar General of Shipping and Seamen who then periodically passed the information to the Registrars General of Births, Deaths and Marriages of England and Wales, Scotland or Ireland as appropriate.

Up until 1889 separate series of Registers were kept for seamen and passengers, but in 1890 a combined series was introduced. The various Registers would typically contain details such as name, rank/occupation, age, date of birth, address, date of death, place of death (often in longitude and latitude), cause of death and name, official number and port of registry of the vessel.

To access a death at sea (if an approximate date of death is known) first examine the index books for the year the death was registered. They are organised by the name of the vessel and of the deceased. Then search in the Death Register for the particular year, under the relevant month. You will find that there is sometimes a delay between a death occurring and the date it was registered.

The National Archives holds copies of the *Registers* and *Index* volumes of *Births, Marriages and Deaths of Passengers and*

Seamen at Sea, 1891-1972 in the Board of Trade files *BT 334*. Later Registers are kept by the Registry of Shipping and Seamen.

When a death at sea occurs on a British vessel, the Master is required to complete a *Return of Death*. These Returns include name, official number and port of registry of the vessel, date and place of death, name, age, rank/occupation, address and cause of death. The reverse of the form includes an extract of the vessel's Log Book, which gives an account of the events, which led to the death at sea. However, these accounts were not always included. *Returns of Death* form the basis of the *Death Registers* described above.

Surviving *Returns of Death*, for the periods 1914-1919 and 1939-1964 are held by the National Maritime Museum. Few Returns have survived for the period 1920-1938. The Registry of Shipping and Seamen holds those from 1990 to date (those between 1965 and 1989 were disposed of).

When a vessel was lost at sea the Log Book would have been lost with the vessel, therefore the owners of the vessel would submit a copy of the crew list to the Registrar General of Shipping and Seamen. These lists would be used for the registration of the deaths of the crew members. Casualties and Deaths Lists are organised by official number of the vessel. These numbers can be located by consulting the annual volumes of the *Lloyd's Register* and the *Mercantile Navy List*.

Casualties and Death Lists, including those from fishing vessels, for the period 1920-1938 are to be found at the National Maritime Museum.

Other useful sources held by The National Archives include the *Inquiry Reports* concerning deaths at sea, 1939-1995 in *BT 341*. These contain statements, Log Book entries, medical reports and other relevant information regarding the particular death at sea, and are organised by year and by ship name. Rolls of Honour of Merchant Navy seamen and Fishing Fleet crews (1939-1945 only) can be found in *BT 339*.

Records of shipping lost at sea are also available for public consultation at The National Archives, the Guildhall Library and the National Maritime Museum.

In addition to the Board of Trade files *BT 110*, at The National Archives, you may find the Ministry of Shipping files *MT 25* helpful as they contain returns and lists of vessels sunk during the First World War, papers on the movement of troops, manning of the Merchant Service, casualties and registration. Records relating to the loss of trawlers for the same period are located in the Admiralty files *ADM 137*. For losses during the Second World War see the Ministry of War Transport files *MT 9, MT 15* and *MT 59*; also the seven volumes of daily casualties to Merchant Shipping (1940-1945) in *BT 347*. In addition, the Admiralty files *ADM 199* contain much material on the loss of individual vessels, including interviews with survivors.

The Guildhall Library holds many excellent sources for information on shipping losses. These include *Missing Vessels Books* for the period 1873-1954, which list those vessels posted 'missing' but whose fate is not known, and the *Lloyd's Loss and Casualty Books*, for the period 1837-1998. Each set of books is accompanied by an index.

The National Maritime Museum holds similar records, including a *Shipwreck Index*, organised by the date of the loss and by the name of the vessel lost.

Reference should also be made to local records and newspapers as they often contain listings and details of casualties from their areas.

COMMONWEALTH WAR GRAVES COMMISSION

The **Commonwealth War Graves Commission, 2 Marlow Road, Maidenhead, Berkshire SL6 7DX** holds details of the burial place or commemoration site for those who died in service during the periods 1914-1921 and 1939-1947.

This organisation was established in May 1917 as the **Imperial War Graves Commission**, but changed its name to the **Commonwealth War Graves Commission** in 1960. The Commission decided that all service personnel would be treated equally, being buried close to where they died and with uniform headstones. These graves would be cared for in perpetuity. Individuals with no known grave would have their names carved on a memorial.

As well as having information on the burial site or place of commemoration, the Commission has details of date of death and the unit to which the individual was attached. Often, details of their home address and next of kin were included.

Details of those employed in the Merchant Navy, who were 'buried at sea' during the First and Second World Wars, are recorded in the memorial registers relating to Tower Hill and Liverpool. However, because of the fact that the Merchant Navy was primarily a civilian service not all Merchant Seamen who died during the wars will automatically have been included. The Commonwealth War Graves Commission has complex criteria for inclusion, but deaths should have been as a result of 'increased war risk' and have been confirmed by the Registrar General of Shipping and Seamen. The Merchant Navy Association is currently campaigning for a memorial to commemorate all Merchant Seamen who died in both world wars.

It is not possible to visit the Commonwealth War Graves Commission in person. The Commission may charge a search fee for postal enquiries, but since information is now computerised, it can be accessed freely via their *Debt of Honour* database available on their website **www.cwgc.org** Copies of all the Commission's published registers are located in the Department of Printed Books' Reading Room and are in regular use.

PUBLISHED CASUALTY LISTS AND ROLLS OF HONOUR

In addition to the set of the **Commonwealth War Graves Commission** memorial and cemetery registers, the Department of Printed Books holds a large collection of operational and shipping histories, some of which include casualties, and a number of published rolls of honour. Of particular importance for confirming basic details, are the volumes of the *Cross of Sacrifice* by SD and DB Jarvis, covering the First World War. The information these volumes contain includes full name, rank, decorations, cause of death, date of death, unit and details of grave or memorial location. The authors have also taken care to cross refer possible misspellings of names. A similar publication for the Second World War is the *Book of Remembrance: the Merchant Navy World War Two* researched by Ian Stockbridge. These volumes and the Commonwealth War Graves Commission registers are available for consultation in our Reading Room.

Our library catalogues can also reveal a rich vein of privately produced rolls of honour for schools, universities, companies, professions and for localities. Of particular interest are the two typescript registers of *Merchant Navy Radio Officers Killed at Sea, 1939-1945*, compiled by Peter J Barber and George V Monk and the *Lloyd's War Losses* volumes which are compilations of shipping casualties drawn from the manuscript records held in the Lloyd's Marine Collection at the Guildhall Library. Also of note are the volumes of the *National Roll of the Great War 1914-1918*. The volumes for Southampton and Portsmouth (Sections IV and X) in particular include references to Merchant Navy personnel. The *National Roll* project was never completed and is far from comprehensive. Paradoxically it can be both unreliable, but at times, an excellent source of personal information. Inclusion was by subscription and the individuals listed included many combatants who returned safely home at the end of the war.

The **United Kingdom National Inventory of War Memorials**, based at the Imperial War Museum, may be able to assist with enquiries concerning memorials for Merchant

Seamen. The Inventory is an information-gathering project, which has created a database of all known war memorials in the United Kingdom, estimated to be in the region of 70,000. This can be consulted by appointment in the Reading Room. The database can be accessed on **www.ukniwm.org.uk** The Inventory, in conjunction with Channel 4, is currently working on a searchable index of names from the First World War. Files containing additional material may be consulted, by prior appointment. The Inventory welcomes information on any memorial currently missing from their records.

ADDITIONAL SOURCES

SHIP AND OPERATIONAL HISTORIES

Operational records, shipping company and individual ships' histories will prove invaluable for background detail. The Department of Printed Books holds copies of the official histories *The Merchant Navy* by Archibald Hurd, *Seaborne Trade* by C Ernest Fayle and *Naval Operations* by Julian S Corbett and Henry Newbolt, all of which give a good insight to maritime operations during the First World War. Facsimile reprints of these publications have been produced by the Department of Printed Books; details can be found in Appendix III. Although no specific 'official histories' have been produced for the Second World War the researcher will find the commercially published volumes *Life Line* by Peter Elphick, *Survivors* by GH and R Bennett and *The Fourth Service* by John Slader give excellent accounts of the varying roles of the Merchant Navy.

The most important, and perhaps the most complex area of the Merchant Navy's involvement in maritime operations revolves around the concept of the convoy. Here, the Department of Printed Books holds a wealth of published accounts relating to Atlantic, Arctic and Mediterranean convoys. A few examples have been listed in the *Select Bibliography* in Appendix III. The definitive book on this subject is the *Allied Convoy System, 1939-1945: Organisation, Defence and Operation* by Arnold Hague, which is invaluable for tracing the movements and composition of all convoys in operation during the period of the Second World War. Also of particular interest is the privately published *SAWAS, 1939-1947 Book of Thanks* edited by Captain EAS Bailey, which lists the code numbers and sailing dates of all convoys sailing from the UK to South Africa, includes the names of the troopships and the escorting naval vessels involved and rolls of honour of the servicemen who perished during these voyages. This is a rare publication printed as a limited edition of only 700 copies. The multi-volume *The War at Sea: Preliminary Narrative*, an unpublished typescript compiled by the Admiralty Naval Staff during the Second World War, is also helpful. This contains many useful references to individual convoys as well as to merchant shipping losses. Another good source of reference for convoy losses is *Axis Submarine Successes, 1939-1945* by Jürgen Rohwer. The Department of Printed Books has compiled select reading lists on the convoys, copies of which are available on request.

Official documentation such as operational records, convoy records and ships' logs are held at **The National Archives**. The most relevant files for operational records relating to the First World War, are the Ministry of Transport files *MT 23* and *MT 25*. Convoy records are to be found in the Admiralty files *ADM 137* and ships' logs in the Board of Trade files *BT 165*. Operational records relating to the Second World War are included in the Ministry of (War) Transport files *MT 40* and *MT 59* with convoy records in Admiralty files *ADM 199* (includes survivors' reports) and *ADM 237*, and ships' logs for the period in *BT 380, BT 381* and *BT 387*. You may also find the Guildhall Library's collection of *Voyage Record Cards* of assistance.

SHIPPING COMPANIES

Records of shipping companies are useful to the researcher as they contain information on the company's employees, as well as details of the fleet and the ships' sailings. The Department of Printed Books holds a good collection of shipping company histories and individual ships' histories although, in the main, they refer to the larger companies such as the Cunard Line, P & O, Union-Castle line and famous vessels like the SS *Lusitania*, SS *Lancastria, Queen Elizabeth* and *Queen Mary*. However, there are many 'smaller' company histories as well as individual ships' histories published in periodicals such as *Sea Breezes: the Magazine of Ships and the Sea* (published by the Mannin Media Group, Media House, Cronkbourne, Douglas, Isle of Man IM4 4SB) and *Marine News: Journal of the World Ship Society* (published by the World Ship Society, c/o the General Secretary, 101 The Everglades, Dukes Meadow Drive, Hempstead, Gillingham, Kent ME7 3PZ). Runs of these periodicals are available for consultation in our Reading Room.

Most of the official records relating to shipping companies have been lodged with the **National Maritime Museum**, the **Guildhall Library**, the **Merseyside Maritime Museum**, the **Glasgow University Archives**, the **Liverpool University Archives** and various other archives and record offices around the country. Details of some of these archives are listed in Appendix II.

The Department of Printed Books does not hold any detailed charts showing sailings or wreck positions other than those reproduced in published histories. Officially produced charts are held by The National Archives and the National Maritime

Museum. In addition, accurate locations for wrecks, particularly off the UK coastlines, may be obtained from the **United Kingdom Hydrographic Office, Admiralty Way, Taunton, Somerset TA1 2DN**. A search fee may be levied.

The Department of Printed Books holds a fair collection of complementary published sources, including titles giving technical background to the ships, armament and training involved, as well as badges, uniforms and medals. We hold runs of the *Lloyd's Register of Shipping* (1914-1940) and the *Mercantile Navy List* (1913-1966). Although incomplete they do help to establish basic facts about individual ships. Periodicals and our collection of autobiographies can also provide unexpected references on differing areas of service with the Merchant Navy.

Researchers are welcome to use any of the collections, by prior appointment, available at the **Imperial War Museum**. The six Collecting Departments of the Museum are: Art, Documents, Exhibits and Firearms, Film and Photograph Archives, Printed Books and the Sound Archive.

The Department of Documents in particular, holds a number of unpublished diaries and memoirs written by officers and crew who served in the Merchant Navy during the First and Second World Wars. A few give a full account of their experiences at sea, but the majority are specifically concerned either with the sinking of their vessel, their capture by the enemy or their participation in particular convoys and other maritime operations. Similar collections are held by the Sound Archive. Their collection of interviews with veterans offer an 'array of experience often recalled with emotional force.' In many cases the Photograph Archive can produce a print of an individual ship. Although there are many photographs of Merchant Seamen, the views tend to be of groups rather than individual portraits.

An *Access Guide* to all the Imperial War Museum collections is available on request, and most departmental catalogues can be consulted as part of the *Collections Online* at **www.iwm.collections.org.uk** Not every item in the Museum has been catalogued on computer and there will inevitably be some omissions, so please make enquiries with the relevant department if you do not find what you are looking for.

Researchers may also be interested in the records of seamen's trade unions, as they too contain some useful references to the seaman's career. Records of the **National Union of Seamen** from 1911 and some branch records of the **British Seafarers' Union**, from 1915, are to be found in the archives of the **University of Warwick, Modern Records Centre, University of Warwick Library, Coventry CV4 7AL**.

For information relating to the nineteenth century and earlier, we would recommend contacting the National Maritime Museum, the Guildhall Library and the Merseyside Maritime Museum. Details of these and other relevant museums and archives are outlined in Appendix II.

PERIODICALS

Periodical publications, including 'old comrades' associations' newsletters often carry information, which will be of interest to the family history researcher. The Department of Printed Books currently receives over 500 periodical titles relating to the Museum's subject field and can advise on those most relevant to a particular enquiry.

GENEALOGICAL SOURCES

There are also many magazines on the market, which offer advice and guidance on family history. The Imperial War Museum has subscribed to *Family Tree Magazine* since 1989 (back copies can be consulted in our Reading Room), but there have been many new publications of this sort produced in recent years. *Family Tree Magazine* is published monthly by **ABM Publishing Ltd, 61 Great Whyte, Ramsey, Huntingdon, Cambridgeshire PE26 1HJ**. Other titles include *Family History News and Digest* produced by the Federation of Family History Societies, *Genealogists Magazine* by the Society of Genealogists, *Ancestors* published by The National Archives and *Family History Monthly*. Contact details for these are to be found in Appendix II.

Genealogical societies such as the **Federation of Family History Societies, c/o FFHS Administrator, PO Box 2425, Coventry CV5 6YX** and the **Society of Genealogists, 14 Charterhouse Buildings, Goswell Road, London EC1M 7BA** are also able to offer advice as well as provide details of local societies and organisations.

Both societies have also produced useful guides for the family historian, some of which are listed in Appendix III.

The Family and Local History Handbook, published annually, is full of genealogical and historical articles of interest to the beginner and experienced researcher alike. It also contains contact details for a wide variety of registrars of births, marriages and deaths, record offices, libraries, museums and societies.

An online listing of record repositories can be found at **www.nationalarchives.gov.uk/archon** The *National Register of Archives*, available online at **www.national archives.gov.uk/nra** will allow some searching of archival catalogues. Details about family and local history resources located in public libraries, together with contact details, can be found at **www.familia.org.uk**

The internet has revolutionised family history research and there are many websites that can help with either a specific subject, contacting individuals or appealing for information. Not everything that appears on the internet is current or correct information and you should always check to see who has created the website and for what purpose. Some website addresses appear in Appendix II, but you should be aware that websites sometimes just disappear and new ones appear all the time. Following links from one site to another can often be a rewarding, if sometimes frustrating activity.

Family History fairs are held regularly around the country and can be excellent places for both beginners and experienced researchers to find out what is available. The Imperial War Museum does at times participate in larger fairs and regularly has family history days in the Museum galleries. Visitors are welcome to come and ask questions and staff are able to spend longer dealing with these than they are in the normal course of their work. Please check the family history pages on the Museum's website for details of these events.

APPENDIX I

ABBREVIATIONS

These are a selection only of the most commonly used abbreviations. The Department of Printed Books holds several published guides to abbreviations in use at various times during the twentieth century.

ADM	Admiralty
ASR	Air Sea Rescue
BSU	British Seafarers' Union
BT	Board of Trade
CAM	Catapult Aircraft Merchantman
CG	Coastguard
CS	Continuous Service
CWGC	Commonwealth War Graves Commission
DEMS	Defensively Equipped Merchant Ships
HMS	His Majesty's Ship/Her Majesty's Ship
IWGC	Imperial War Graves Commission
LR	Lloyd's Register
MAC	Merchant ship Aircraft Carrier
MFA	Merchant Fleet Auxiliary
MM	Mercantile Marine/Merchant Marine
MMR	Merchant Marine Reserve
MN	Merchant Navy
MNL	Mercantile Navy List
MOD	Ministry of Defence
MS	Merchant Service
MT	Ministry of (War) Transport
MV	Motor Vessel
NA	National Archives (formerly the Public Record Office)
POW	Prisoner of War

PRO	Public Record Office
RFA	Royal Fleet Auxiliary
RGSS	Registrar General of Shipping and Seamen
RN	Royal Navy/Royal Naval
RND	Royal Naval Division
RNH	Royal Naval Hospital
RNPS	Royal Naval Patrol Service
RNR	Royal Naval Reserve
RNR (T)	Royal Naval Reserve Trawler Section
RNVR	Royal Naval Volunteer Reserve
RNV (S) R	Royal Naval Volunteer Supplementary Reserve
RSS	Registry of Shipping and Seamen
SS	Steamship/Sailing Ship
TNA	The National Archives (formerly the Public Record Office)
Yt	Yacht

RANKS AND TITLES

A	Apprentice
AB	Able Seaman
AS	Steward
B	Boatswain (Bo'sun)
C	Captain
Cd	Commissioned
Cdr	Commander
Cdre	Commodore
Cdt	Cadet
CE	Chief Engineer
Cf M	Chief Mate
Ck	Cook
Cr	Carpenter
CS	Chief Steward
DH	Deck Hand
E	Engineer
F	Fireman

Gr	Gunner
M	Mate
2M	Second Mate
3M	Third Mate
MO	Medical Officer
Mr	Master
OS	Ordinary Seaman
P	Purser
QM	Quartermaster
S	Seaman
Sg	Surgeon
Skr	Skipper
Sl Mkr	Sailmaker
St	Stoker
Tr	Trimmer
WO	Wireless Operator
WTO	Wireless Telegraphy Operator

HONOURS AND AWARDS

AM	Albert Medal
AM (B)	Albert Medal in Bronze
AM (G)	Albert Medal in Gold
BEM	British Empire Medal
BEM (Gall)	British Empire Medal (specifically for gallantry)
CB	Companion of the Order of the Bath
CBE	Commander of the Order of the British Empire
Commendn	Commendation
DCM	Distinguished Conduct Medal
DSC	Distinguished Service Cross
DSM	Distinguished Service Medal
DSO	Companion of the Distinguished Service Order
EGM	Empire Gallantry Medal
GC	George Cross

GM	George Medal
KBE	Knight Commander of the Order of the British Empire
KCB	Knight Commander of the Order of the Bath
KG	Knight of the Order of the Garter
LS&GCM	Long Service and Good Conduct Medal
MBE	Member of the Order of the British Empire
MBE (Gall)	Member of the Order of the British Empire (specifically for gallantry)
MID	Mention-in-Despatches
OBE	Officer of the Order of the British Empire
RRC	Member of the Order of the Royal Red Cross
RRC Bar	Bar to the Royal Red Cross
SGM	Sea Gallantry Medal
VC	Victoria Cross

APPENDIX II

ADDRESSES

Listed below are details of some museums, archives and record offices, which may be able to offer assistance with family history enquiries. Please note that it is always advisable to contact an institution in advance of an intended visit in order to check on the availability of material relating to your particular enquiry and confirm opening hours. Those with internet access will find that many institutions now have their own website which outline their holdings, arrangements for public access and details of any search fees and/or charges which may be levied. Information on other museums and archives can be found in the annual publications the *World of Learning* and the *Museums and Galleries Yearbook*, available at most libraries and information centres.

RECORD OFFICES

Bristol Record Office
'B' Bond Warehouse, Smeaton Road, Bristol BS1 6XN
Tel: 0117 922 4224
www.bristol-city.gov.uk/recordoffice

Commonwealth War Graves Commission
2 Marlow Road, Maidenhead, Berkshire SL6 7DX
Tel: 01628 634221
www.cwgc.org

Data Protection Cell
Director Naval Career Management, Building 1/152, Victory View, HM Naval
Base, Portsmouth, Hampshire PO1 3PX

Family Records Centre
1 Myddelton Street, London EC1R 1UW
Tel: 020 8392 5300
www.familyrecords.gov.uk/frc/

General Register Office (Dublin)
Government Offices, Convent Road, Roscommon, Eire
Tel: 090 6632900
www.groireland.ie

General Register Office (Northern Ireland)
Oxford House, 49-55 Chichester Street, Belfast, Northern Ireland BT1 4HL
Tel: 028 9025 2000
www.groni.gov.uk

General Register Office for Scotland
New Register House, 3 West Register Street,
Edinburgh, Scotland EH1 3YT
Tel: 0131 334 0380
www.gro-scotland.gov.uk

Corporation of Lloyd's
Council Secretariat, 1 Lime Street, London EC3M 7HA
[possible source of citations for Lloyd's Medals for Gallantry at Sea,
especially recent awards]

The National Archives
Ruskin Avenue, Kew, Richmond, Surrey TW9 4DU
Tel: 020 8876 3444
www.nationalarchives.gov.uk

National Archives of Ireland
Bishop Street, Dublin 8, Eire
Tel: 35301 407 2300
www.nationalarchives.ie

The National Archives of Scotland
HM General Register House, 2 Princes Street,
Edinburgh, Scotland EH1 3YY
Tel: 0131 535 1334
www.nas.gov.uk

Naval Secretary (Honours and Awards)
Room G10, Fleet Headquarters, West Battery, Whale Island, Portsmouth,
Hampshire PO2 8DX

Navy Search
TNT Archive Services, Tetron Point, William Nadin Way,
Swadlincote, Derbyshire DE11 0BB

Public Record Office of Northern Ireland
66 Balmoral Avenue, Belfast, Northern Ireland BT9 6NY
Tel: 028 9025 5905
www.proni.gov.uk

Registry of Shipping and Seamen
MCA Cardiff, Anchor Court, Keen Road,
Cardiff CF24 5JW
Tel: 029 2044 8800
www.mcga.gov.uk

United Kingdom Hydrographic Office
Admiralty Way, Taunton, Somerset TA1 2DN
Tel: 01823 337900
www.ukho.gov.uk

MUSEUMS, LIBRARIES AND ARCHIVES

Bristol City Museum and Art Gallery
Queens Road, Bristol BS8 1RL
Tel: 0117 922 3571
www.bristol-city.gov.uk

British Empire and Commonwealth Museum
Clock Tower Yard, Temple Meads, Bristol BS1 6QH
Tel: 0117 925 4980
www.empiremuseum.co.uk

British Library, Newspaper Library
Colindale Avenue, London NW9 5HE
Tel: 020 7412 7353
www.bl.uk/collections/newspapers.html

British Library, Oriental and India Office Collections
96 Euston Road, London NW1 2DB
Tel: 020 7412 7873
www.bl.uk/collections/orientaloffice.html
[Records of the East India Company and some Merchant Navy personnel]

British Red Cross Museum and Archives
44 Moorfields, Moorgate, London EC2Y 9AL
Tel: 020 7877 7058
www.redcross.org.uk

Glasgow Archives and Special Collections
Mitchell Library, North Street, Glasgow G3 7DN
Tel: 0141 287 2910
www.glasgow.gov.uk
[Records of some local shipping companies i.e. Elder Dempster Line]

Glasgow University Archives
13 Thurso Street, Glasgow G11 6PE
Tel: 0141 330 5515
www.archives.gla.ac.uk
[Records of some local shipping companies i.e.
Anchor Line and Ellerman Line]

Guildhall Library, Lloyd's Marine Collection
Aldermanbury, London EC2P 2EJ
Tel: 020 7332 1868
www.cityoflondon.gov.uk

Hartlepool Museum Service
Sir William Gray House, Clarence Road, Hartlepool TS24 8BT
Tel: 01429 523438
www.hartlepool.gov.uk

Hull Maritime Museum

Queen Victoria Square, Hull HU1 3DX

Tel: 01482 613908

www.hullcc.gov.uk

Liverpool University

University of Liverpool Library, Sydney Jones Library, Chatham Street, Liverpool L69 3DA

Tel: 0151 794 2673

www.liv.ac.uk/library/

[Records of local shipping companies i.e. Cunard]

Lloyd's Register of Shipping

71 Fenchurch Street, London EC3M 4BS

Tel: 020 7709 9166

www.lr.org

Lowestoft and East Suffolk Maritime Museum

Sparrows Nest Gardens, Whapload Road, Lowestoft, Suffolk NR32 1XG

Tel: 01502 561963

Marine Society and Sea Cadets

202 Lambeth Road, London SE1 7JW

Tel: 020 7654 7000

www.marine-society.org

Maritime History Archive

Memorial University of Newfoundland, St John's, Newfoundland, A1C 5S7

Tel: 001709 737 8428

www.mun.ca/mha

Merchant Navy Association

National Office, 9 Saxon Way, Caistor,

Market Rasen LN7 6SG

Tel: 01472 851130

www.mna.org.uk

Merseyside Maritime Museum

Archives and Library, Albert Dock, Liverpool L3 4AQ

www.liverpoolmuseums.org.uk/maritime/

National Library of Wales

Aberystwyth, Ceredigion, Wales SY23 3BU

Tel: 01970 623800

www.llgc.org.uk

National Maritime Museum

Romney Road, Greenwich, London SE10 9NF

Tel: 020 8858 4422

www.nmm.ac.uk

Southampton Archives

Southampton City Council, South Block, Civic Centre,

Southampton SO14 7LY

Tel: 023 8083 2251

www.southampton.gov.uk

University of Warwick

Modern Records Centre, University of Warwick Library,

Coventry CV4 7AL

Tel: 024 7652 4219

www.warwick.ac.uk

[Records of Merchant Seamen's trade unions]

MAGAZINES

Marine News: Journal of the World Ship Society
c/o General Secretary, 101 The Everglades, Dukes Meadow Drive,
Hempstead, Gillingham, Kent ME7 3PZ
www.worldshipsociety.org

Sea Breezes: the Magazine of Ships and the Sea
Mannin Media Group, Media House, Cronkbourne, Douglas, Isle of Man
IM4 4SB
Tel: 01624 696573
www.seabreezes.co.im

GENEALOGY

Ancestors
PO Box 38, Richmond TW9 4AJ
Tel: 020 8392 5370
www.ancestorsmagazine.co.uk

Family History Monthly
The Metropolis Group, 140 Wales Farm Road
London W3 6UG
Tel: 0870 732 8080
www.metropolis.co.uk/familyhistory.html

Family Tree Magazine
ABM Publishing Ltd, 61 Great Whyte, Ramsey,
Huntingdon, Cambridgeshire PE26 1HJ
Tel: 01487 814050
www.family-tree.co.uk

Federation of Family History Societies

FFHS Administrator, PO Box 2425, Coventry CV5 6YX

[Publishes *Family History News and Digest*]

www.ffhs.org.uk

Practical Family History

ABM Publishing Ltd, 61 Great Whyte, Ramsey,

Huntingdon, Cambridgeshire PE26 1HJ

Tel: 01487 814050

www.family-tree.co.uk

Society of Genealogists

14 Charterhouse Buildings, Goswell Road, London EC1M 7BA

[Publishes *Genealogists Magazine*]

Tel: 020 7251 8799

www.sog.org.uk

Your Family Tree

Future Publishing, 30 Monmouth Street, Bath BA1 2BW

Tel: 01225 442244

www.futurenet.com/yourfamilytree/

ADDITIONAL WEBSITES

ARCHON (Archives Online)

www.nationalarchives.gov.uk/archon/

British Merchant Navy

www.merchant-navy.net

Familia: the UK and Ireland's Guide to Genealogical Resources in Public Libraries

www.familia.org.uk

Family Records Consortium

www.familyrecords.gov.uk

Gazettes Online

www.gazettes-online.co.uk

Marine Society

www.marine-society.org

Maritime and Coastguard Agency

www.mcga.gov.uk

Maritime Britain

www.maritimebritain.org.uk

Merchant Navy Association

www.mna.org.uk

Merchant Navy Officers

www.merchantnavyofficers.com

National Register of Archives

www.nationalarchives.gov.uk/nra

Port Cities UK

www.portcities.org.uk

Port: Maritime Information Gateway

www.port.nmm.ac.uk

The Red Duster

www.red-duster.co.uk

World Ship Society

www.worldshipsociety.org

APPENDIX III

SELECT BIBLIOGRAPHY

Below are listed a selection of published sources and material held by the Department of Printed Books. These may be consulted in our Reading Room by prior appointment; please give at least 24 hours notice of arrival. In addition, specific subject bibliographies and information sheets are available on request. Please note that we have not attempted to list the many periodical titles that are relevant to maritime research, but we are happy to advise on specific titles where applicable.

Many of these recommended publications will also be available through your local public library or bookseller and in the case of the 'out of print' volumes through second-hand and specialist dealers.

For ease of use, the list has been broken down into the following main subject areas to reflect the different sections in this booklet: Genealogy, Family History, Service Records and Archival Guides (p.65); Medals and Awards (p.68); Casualties and Rolls of Honour (p.70); Maritime Operations in the Twentieth Century (p.75); Merchant Shipping Companies and their Ships (p.82); Life in the Merchant Navy (p.87).

GENEALOGY, FAMILY HISTORY, SERVICE RECORDS AND ARCHIVAL GUIDES

The National Archives have produced a series of helpful leaflets on a variety of subjects. These can be found on their website at **www.nationalarchives.gov.uk/catalogue/researchguides index.asp**

BARRISKILL, DT
A Guide to the Lloyd's Marine Collection and Related Marine Sources at the Guildhall Library compiled by DT Barriskill.
Guildhall Library, London, 1994.
(Guildhall Library Research Guide; 7)
ISBN 0-900422-37-8 (pbk.)

BECKETT, Ian FW
The First World War: the Essential Guide to Sources in the UK National Archives by Ian FW Beckett.
Public Record Office, Richmond, Surrey, 2002.
ISBN 1-903365-41-4

BEVAN, Amanda
Tracing your Ancestors in the Public Record Office by Amanda Bevan.
6th rev. ed.; Public Record Office, Richmond, Surrey, 2002.
(Public Record Office Handbook; no. 19)
ISBN 1-903365-34-1 (pbk.)

BLATCHFORD, Robert
The Family and Local History Handbook: incorporating the Genealogical Services Directory edited and compiled by Robert Blatchford.
9th ed.; Robert Blatchford Publishing, York, 2005.
ISBN 0-95302977-8 (pbk.)

CANTWELL, JD

The Second World War: a Guide to Documents in the Public Record Office by JD Cantwell.

2nd ed.; Public Record Office, Richmond, Surrey, 1998.

(Public Record Office Handbook; no. 15)

ISBN 1-873162-60-X (pbk.)

COLWELL, Stella

The Family Records Centre: a User's Guide by Stella Colwell.

Public Record Office, Richmond, Surrey, 2002.

(Public Record Office Readers' Guide; no. 17)

ISBN 1-903365-36-8 (pbk.)

COX, Jane

New to Kew? by Jane Cox.

Public Record Office, Richmond, Surrey, 1997.

(Public Record Office Readers' Guide; no. 16)

ISBN 1-873162-40-5 (pbk.)

FOSTER, Janet

British Archives: a Guide to Archive Resources in the United Kingdom by Janet Foster and Julia Sheppard.

[Rev. ed.]; Macmillan, London, 1995.

ISBN 0-333-532-554

HARVEY, Richard

A Guide to Genealogical Sources in Guildhall Library compiled by Richard Harvey.

Guildhall Library, London, 1997.

(Guildhall Library Research Guide; 1)

ISBN 0-900422-41-6 (pbk.)

HOGG, Peter L

Basic Facts about ... Using Merchant Ship Records for Family Historians by Peter L Hogg.

Federation of Family History Societies, Bury, Lancashire, 1999.

ISBN 1-86006-045-5 (pbk.)

IMPERIAL WAR MUSEUM

Tracing Your Family History: Royal Navy.

Imperial War Museum, London, 2005.

ISBN 1-901623-36-X (pbk.)

SMITH, Kelvin

Records of Merchant Shipping and Seamen by Kelvin Smith, Christopher T Watts and Michael J Watts.

Public Record Office, Richmond, Surrey, 1998.

ISBN 1-873-162-49-9 (pbk.)

WATTS, Christopher T

My Ancestor was a Merchant Seamen: How can I Find out More about Him? by Christopher T Watts and Michael J Watts.

Society of Genealogists, London, 2004.

ISBN 0-901878-73-1 (pbk.)

WATTS, Christopher T

Tracing Births, Deaths and Marriages at Sea by Christopher T and Michael J Watts.

Society of Genealogists, London, 2004.

ISBN 1-903462-82-7 (pbk.)

MEDALS AND AWARDS

ABBOTT, PE
British Gallantry Awards by PE Abbott and JMA Tamplin.
Nimrod Dix, London, 1981.
ISBN 0-85112-173-X

BROWN, George A
Lloyd's War Medal for Bravery at Sea by George A Brown.
Western Canadian Distributors, Langley, British
Columbia, 1992.
ISBN 0-94813-65-5 [sic]

DICKSON, Bill Chatterton
Seedie's List of Awards to the Merchant Navy for World War II compiled by
Bill Chatterton Dickson.
Ripley Registers, Tisbury, Wiltshire, 1997.
ISBN 0-9513380-4-8

DICKSON, Bill Chatterton
Seedie's Roll of Naval Honours and Awards, 1939-1959 compiled by
Bill Chatterton Dickson.
Ripley Registers, Tisbury, Wiltshire, 1989.
ISBN 0-9513380-0-5

DORLING, H Taprell
Ribbons and Medals by H Taprell Dorling; edited and revised by
Alec A Purves.
Osprey, London, 1983.
ISBN 0-85045-516-2

DYMOND, Steve
Researching British Military Medals: a Practical Guide by Steve Dymond.
Crowood Press, Marlborough, Wiltshire, 1999.
ISBN 1-86126-282-5

FEVYER, WH
The Distinguished Service Cross, 1901-1938 by WH Fevyer.
London Stamp Exchange, London, 1991.
ISBN 0-948130-63-6

FEVYER, WH
The Distinguished Service Medal, 1914-1920 compiled by WH Fevyer.
Hayward, London, 1982.
ISBN 0-903754-97-5

FEVYER, WH
The Distinguished Service Medal, 1939-1946 compiled by WH Fevyer.
Hayward, London, 1981.
ISBN 0-903754-90-8

GOULD, Robert W
British Campaign Medals: Waterloo to the Gulf by Robert W Gould.
4th rev. ed.; Arms and Armour Press, London, 1994.
ISBN 1-85409-224-3

The Register of the George Cross.
This England Books, Cheltenham, 1985.
ISBN 0-906324-06-8

The Register of the Victoria Cross.
Rev. ed.; This England Books, Cheltenham, 1988.
ISBN 0-906324-07-6

SCARLETT, RJ

Under Hazardous Circumstances: a Register of Awards of Lloyd's War Medal for Bravery at Sea, 1939-1945 by RJ Scarlett.

Naval and Military Press, Dallington, Sussex, 1992.

ISBN 0-948130-49-0

CASUALTIES AND ROLLS OF HONOUR

SHIPS' LOSSES

British Vessels Lost at Sea, 1914-18 and 1939-45:

[facsimile reprint of four HMSO publications ...]

Patrick Stephens, Wellingborough, Northants., 1988.

ISBN 1-85260-134-5

HOCKING, Charles

Dictionary of Disasters at Sea during the Age of Steam ... 1824-1962

[2 volumes] by Charles Hocking.

Lloyd's, London, 1969.

HOOKE, Norman

Modern Shipping Disasters, 1963-1987 by Norman Hooke.

Lloyd's, London, 1989.

ISBN 1-85044-211-8

Lloyd's War Losses: the First World War: Casualties to Shipping through Enemy Causes, 1914-1918.

Lloyd's, London, 1990.

ISBN 1-85044-314-9

Lloyd's War Losses: the Second World War. Volume I: British, Allied and Neutral Merchant Vessels Sunk or Destroyed by War Causes.
Lloyd's, London, 1989.
ISBN 1-85044-314-9

Lloyd's War Losses: the Second World War. Volume II: Statistics, Vessels Disappeared, Losses, Without Trace, Badly Damaged, Naval Losses, British, Allied and Neutral Warship Losses, Vessels Sunk by Mines after the War.
Lloyd's, London, 1991.
ISBN 1-85044-412-9

Lloyd's War Losses: the Second World War. Volume III: Vessels Lost or Damaged by War Causes while under Control of German, Italian or other European Axis Powers [2 parts].
[Lloyd's, London], n.d.

TENNANT, AJ
British Merchant Ships Sunk by U-Boats in the 1914-1918 War by AJ Tennant.
Starling Press, Newport, Gwent, 1990.
ISBN 0-9516314-0-3 (pbk.)

WILLIAMS, David
Wartime Disasters at Sea: every Passenger Ship Loss in World War I and II by David Williams.
Patrick Stephens, Yeovil, Somerset, 1997.
ISBN 1-85260-565-0

YOUNG, John M
Britain's Sea War: a Diary of Ship Losses, 1939-1945 by John M Young.
Patrick Stephens, Wellingborough, Northants., 1989.
ISBN 1-85260-042-X

ROLLS OF HONOUR

BARBER, Peter J
British and Commonwealth Radio Officers of the British Merchant Marine Lost at Sea, 1939-1945: Complete Alphabetical and Ship Register compiled by Peter J Barber and George V Monk.
[N.pub., n. p.], 1998.

BARBER, Peter J
Memorial-Register: British Merchant Navy Radio Officers Killed at Sea, 1939-1945 by Peter J Barber.
[PJ Barber, n.p., 1990].

CRABB, Brian James
Beyond the Call of Duty: the Loss of British Commonwealth Mercantile and Service Women at Sea during the Second World War by Brian James Crabb.
Shaun Tyas, Donington, Lincolnshire, 2006.
ISBN 1-900289-66-0

JARVIS, SD
Cross of Sacrifice, Volume 2: Officers who Died in the Service of the Royal Navy, Royal Naval Reserve, Royal Naval Volunteer Reserve, Royal Marines, Royal Naval Air Service and Royal Air Force, 1914-1919 by SD Jarvis and DB Jarvis.
Roberts Medals, Reading, Berkshire, 1993.
ISBN 1-873058-31-4

JARVIS, SD
Cross of Sacrifice, Volume 4: Non-commissioned Officers and Men of the Royal Navy, Royal Flying Corps and Royal Air Force, 1914-1919 by SD Jarvis and DB Jarvis.
Roberts Medals, Reading, Berkshire, 1996.
ISBN 1-873058-41-1

JARVIS, SD

Cross of Sacrifice, Volume 5: the Officers, Men and Women of the Merchant Navy and Mercantile Fleet Auxiliary, 1914-1919 by SD Jarvis and DB Jarvis.
Naval and Military Press, Uckfield, East Sussex, 2000.
ISBN 1-897632-03-7

National Roll of the Great War, 1914-1918. Sections I-XV.
National Publishing, London, [1920-1922?].
[Complete set held by IWM – includes recently compiled index volume]

STOCKBRIDGE, Ian

Book of Remembrance: the Merchant Navy World War Two researched by Ian Stockbridge.
NUMAST, [London, 2003?].

MEDICAL

MELLOR, W Franklin

Casualties and Medical Statistics edited by W Franklin Mellor.
HMSO, London, 1972.
(History of the Second World War: United Kingdom Medical Series)
ISBN 0-11-320997-5

MITCHELL, TJ

Medical Services: Casualties and Medical Statistics of the Great War by TJ Mitchell.
HMSO, London, 1931.
(History of the Great War: Based on Official Documents)
[The Imperial War Museum, Department of Printed Books produced a reprint of this volume in 1997.
ISBN 1-870423-28-3]

MEMORIALS

GIBSON, Edwin

Courage Remembered: the Story Behind the Construction and Maintenance of the Commonwealth Military Cemeteries and Memorials of the Wars of 1914-1918 and 1939-1945 by Edwin Gibson and G Kingsley Ward.
HMSO, London, 1989.
ISBN 0-11-772608-7

QUINLAN, Mark

British War Memorials by Mark Quinlan.
Authors On Line, Hertford, 2005.
ISBN 0-7552-0186-8 (pbk.)

QUINLAN, Mark

Remembrance by Mark Quinlan.
Authors On Line, Hertford, 2005.
ISBN 0-7552-0157-4 (pbk.)

SAUNDERS, David

Britain's Maritime Memorials and Mementoes by David Saunders.
Patrick Stephens, Sparkford, Somerset, 1996.
ISBN 1-85260-466-2

MARITIME OPERATIONS IN THE TWENTIETH CENTURY

GENERAL WORKS

ALBION, Robert Greenhalgh
Naval and Maritime History: an Annotated Bibliography by Robert Greenhalgh Albion.
4th ed.; David and Charles, Newton Abbot, Devon, 1973.
ISBN 0-7153-6007-8

DOUGHTY, Martin
Merchant Shipping and War: a Study in Defence Planning in Twentieth-Century Britain by Martin Doughty.
Royal Historical Society, London, 1982.
ISBN 0-901050-83-0

EVANS, Clayton
Rescue at Sea: an International History of Lifesaving, Coastal Rescue Craft and Organisations by Clayton Evans.
Conway Maritime Press, London, 2003.
ISBN 0-85177-934-4

HOPE, Ronald
The Merchant Navy by Ronald Hope.
Stanford Maritime, London, 1980.
ISBN 0-540-07335-0

LABAREE, Benjamin Woods
A Supplement (1971-1986) to Robert G Albion's Naval and Maritime History: an Annotated Bibliography by Benjamin W Labaree.
4th ed.; Mystic Seaport Museum, Mystic, Connecticut, 1988.
ISBN 0-913372-46-3 (pbk.)

WARNER, Oliver

*The Life-Boat Service: a History of the Royal National Life-Boat Institution,
1824-1974* by Oliver Warner.

Cassell, London, 1974.

ISBN 0-304-29061-0

WEBB, William

Coastguard!: an Official History of HM Coastguard by William Webb.

HMSO, London, 1976.

ISBN 0-11-510675-8

FIRST WORLD WAR

CORBETT, Julian S

Naval Operations [5 volumes and 4 map cases] by Julian S Corbett
and Henry Newbolt.

Longmans, Green, London, [1921-1931].

(History of the Great War: Based on Official Documents)

[The Imperial War Museum, Department of Printed Books produced
reprints of these volumes between 1995 and 1997. A paperback reprint
also became available in 2003.]

FAYLE, C Ernest

Seaborne Trade [3 volumes] by C Ernest Fayle.

John Murray, London, [1920-1924].

(History of the Great War: Based on Official Documents)

[The Imperial War Museum, Department of Printed Books produced a
reprint of these volumes in 1997.]

GIBSON, RH

The German Submarine War, 1914-1918 by RH Gibson and Maurice Prendergast.

Constable, London, 1931.

[A paperback reprint became available in 2003.

ISBN 1-843425-35-1 (pbk.)]

HURD, Archibald

The Merchant Navy [3 volumes] by Archibald Hurd.

John Murray, London, [1921-1929].

(History of the Great War: Based on Official Documents)

[A paperback reprint became available in 2003]

SECOND WORLD WAR

ADMIRALTY. NAVAL STAFF. TORPEDO AND STAFF DUTIES DIVISION

The War at Sea, September 1939-September 1945: Preliminary Narrative compiled by the Admiralty, Naval Staff, Torpedo and Staff Duties Division.

[Admiralty, London, 1944-1946].

BEHRENS, CBA

Merchant Shipping and the Demands of War by CBA Behrens.

HMSO, London, 1955.

(History of the Second World War: United Kingdom Civil Series)

EDWARDS, Bernard

The Fighting Tramps: the British Merchant Navy goes to War by Bernard Edwards.

Hale, London, 1989.

ISBN 0-7090-3702-3

ELPHICK, Peter
Life Line: the Merchant Navy at War, 1939-45 by Peter Elphick.
Chatham Publishing, London, 1999.
ISBN 1-86176-100-7

HAY, Doddy
War Under the Red Ensign: the Merchant Navy, 1939-45 by Doddy Hay.
Jane's, London, 1982.
ISBN 0-7106-0205-7

LEWIS, William J
Under the Red Duster: the Merchant Navy in World War II by William J Lewis.
Airlife, Shrewsbury, 2003.
ISBN 1-84037-383-0

ROHWER, Jürgen
Axis Submarine Successes, 1939-1945 by Jürgen Rohwer.
Patrick Stephens, Cambridge, 1983.
ISBN 0-85059-695-5

ROSKILL, SW
The War at Sea, 1939-1945 [4 volumes] by SW Roskill.
HMSO, London, [1954-1961].
(History of the Second World War: United Kingdom Military Series)
[A paperback reprint became available in 2004.]

SLADER, John
The Fourth Service: Merchantmen at War, 1939-1945 by John Slader.
Robert Hale, London, 1994.
ISBN 0-7090-4848-3

SLADER, John
The Red Duster at War: a History of the Merchant Navy during the Second World War by John Slader.
William Kimber, London, 1988.
ISBN 0-7183-0679-1

WOODMAN, Richard
The Real Cruel Sea: the Merchant Navy in the Battle of the Atlantic 1939-1943 by Richard Woodman.
John Murray, London, 2005.
ISBN 0-7195-6599-5 (pbk.)

CONVOYS

BAILEY, EAS
SAWAS, 1939-1947: Book of Thanks, 1980 [3 volumes] edited by Captain EAS Bailey ... [et al].
EAS Bailey, Inversanda, Ardgour, by Fort William, 1981-1983.
ISBN 0-9507481-0-2

BURN, Alan
The Fighting Commodores: the Convoy Commanders in the Second World War by Alan Burn.
Leo Cooper, Barnsley, South Yorkshire, 1999.
ISBN 0-85052-504-7

EDWARDS, Bernard
Attack and Sink!: the Battle for Convoy SC.42 by Bernard Edwards.
New Guild, Wimborne Minster, Dorset, 1995.
ISBN 1-89969-440-4 (pbk.)

HAGUE, Arnold
The Allied Convoy System, 1939-1945: Organization, Defence and Operation by Arnold Hague.
Chatham Publishing, London, 2000.
ISBN 1-86176-147-3

HAGUE, Arnold
Convoy Rescue Ships: a History of the Rescue Service, its Ships and their Crews, 1940-1945 by Arnold Hague.
World Ship Society, Gravesend, Kent, 1998.
ISBN 0-90-5617-88-6 (pbk.)

HASKELL, WA
Shadows on the Horizon: the Battle of Convoy HX-233 by WA Haskell.
Chatham Publishing, London, 1998.
ISBN 1-86176-081-7

MIDDLEBROOK, Martin
Convoy: the Battle for Convoy SC.122 and HX.229 by Martin Middlebrook.
Allen Lane, London, 1976.
ISBN 0-7139-0927-7

SMITH, Peter C
Arctic Victory: the Story of Convoy PQ.18 by Peter C Smith.
Kimber, London, 1975.
ISBN 0-7183-0074-2

SMITH, Peter C
Pedestal: the Malta Convoy of August 1942 by Peter C Smith.
2nd rev. ed.; Kimber, London, 1987.
ISBN 0-7183-0632-5

THOMAS, David A
The Atlantic Star, 1939-1945 by David A Thomas.
WH Allen, London, 1990.
ISBN 1-85227-147-7

THOMAS, David A
Malta Convoys, 1940-42: the Struggle at Sea by David A Thomas.
Leo Cooper, Barnsley, South Yorkshire, 1999.
ISBN 0-85052-663-9

WINTON, John
Convoy: the Defence of Sea Trade, 1890-1990 by John Winton.
Michael Joseph, London, 1983.
ISBN 0-7181-2163-5

WOODMAN, Richard
The Arctic Convoys, 1941-1945 by Richard Woodman.
John Murray, London, 1994.
ISBN 0-7195-5079-3

WOODMAN, Richard
Malta Convoys, 1940-1943 by Richard Woodman.
John Murray, London, 2000.
ISBN 0-7195-5753-4

MERCHANT SHIPPING COMPANIES AND THEIR SHIPS

SHIPPING COMPANIES

COWDEN, James E
The Price of Peace: Elder Dempster, 1939-1945 by James E Cowden.
Jocast, Liverpool, 1981.
ISBN 0-9507480-0-5 (pbk.)

CUBBIN, Graeme
Harrisons of Liverpool: a Chronicle of Ships and Men 1830-2002 by
Graeme Cubbin.
World Ship Society, Gravesend, Kent, 2003.
ISBN 1-901703-48-7

HEATON, PM
The Abbey Line: History of a Cardiff Shipping Venture by PM Heaton.
PM Heaton, Pontypool, Gwent, 1983.
ISBN 0-950-7714-2-2

HOWARTH, David
The Story of P and O: the Peninsular and Oriental Steam Navigation Company
by David Howarth and Stephen Howarth.
Weidenfeld and Nicolson, London, 1986.
ISBN 0-297-78965-1

MCCART, Neil
Atlantic Liners of the Cunard Line: from 1884 to the Present Day by Neil
McCart.
Patrick Stephens, Wellingborough, Northants., 1990.
ISBN 1-85260-065-9

MURRAY, Marischal

Union-Castle Chronicle, 1853-1953 by Marischal Murray.

Longmans, Green, London, 1953.

RABSON, Stephen

P and O: a Fleet History by Stephen Rabson and Kevin O'Donoghue.

World Ship Society, Kendal, Cumbria, 1988.

ISBN 0-905617-45-2

SHIPPING

GENERAL

JORDAN, Roger W

*The World's Merchant Fleets 1939: the Particulars and Wartime Fates
of 6000 Ships* by Roger W Jordan.

Chatham Publishing, London, 1999.

ISBN 1-86176-023-X

Lloyd's Register of Shipping.

Lloyd's, London.

Annual publication.

[Printed Books holdings, from 1914-1940, are incomplete.]

The Mercantile Navy List and Maritime Directory.

HMSO, London.

Annual publication.

[Printed Books holdings, from 1914-1966, are incomplete.]

MILLER, William H

Transatlantic Liners at War: the Story of the Queens by William H Miller and David F Hutchings.

David and Charles, Newton Abbot, 1985.

ISBN 0-7153-8511-9

MITCHELL, WH

British Standard Ships of World War I by WH Mitchell and LA Sawyer.

Sea Breezes, Liverpool, 1968.

MITCHELL, WH

The Empire Ships: a Record of British-Built and Acquired Merchant Ships During the Second World War by WH Mitchell and LA Sawyer.

2nd ed.; Lloyds of London Press, London, 1990.

ISBN 1-85044-275-4

OSBORNE, Richard

Conversion for War edited by Dr Richard Osborne.

World Ship Society, Kendal, 1983.

ISBN 0-905617-25-8 (pbk.)

PLUMMER, Russell

The Ships that Saved an Army: a Comprehensive Record of the 1300 'Little Ships' of Dunkirk by Russell Plummer.

Patrick Stephens, Wellingborough, Northants., 1990.

ISBN 1-85260-210-4

INDIVIDUAL

BARKER, Ralph
Children of the Benares: a War Crime and its Victims by Ralph Barker.
Methuen, London, 1987.
ISBN 0-413-42310-7

BROWNING, Marion
Uganda: the Story of a Very Special Ship by Marion Browning ... [et al].
SS Uganda Trust, Broadstone, Dorset, 1998.
ISBN 0-9531082-0-1

Canberra: the Great White Whale.
Patrick Stephens, Cambridge, 1983.
ISBN 0-85059-636-X

CRABB, Brian James
The Forgotten Tragedy: the Story of the Sinking of HMT Lancastria by
Brian James Crabb.
Shaun Tyas, Donington, Lincolnshire, 2002.
ISBN 1-900289-50-4

GROSSMITH, Frederick
The Sinking of the Laconia: a Tragedy in the Battle of the Atlantic by
Frederick Grossmith.
Paul Watkins, Stamford, 1994.
ISBN 1-871615-68-2

HARDING, Steve
Gray Ghost: the RMS Queen Mary at War by Steve Harding.
Pictorial Histories Publishing, Missoula, Montana, 1982.
ISBN 0-933126-26-3 (pbk.)

HICKEY, Des
Seven Days to Disaster: the Sinking of the Lusitania by Des Hickey and Gus Smith.
Collins, London, 1981.
ISBN 0-00-216882-0

KONINGS, Chris
Queen Elizabeth at War: His Majesty's Transport, 1939-1946 by Chris Konings.
Patrick Stephens, Wellingborough, Northants., 1985.
ISBN 0-85059-725-0

PRESTON, Diana
Wilful Murder: the Sinking of the Lusitania by Diana Preston.
Doubleday, London, 2002.
ISBN 0-385-60173-5

STEELE, James
Queen Mary by James Steele.
Phaidon Press, London, 1995.
ISBN 0-7148-2891-2

THOMAS, David A
Queen Mary and the Cruiser: the Curacoa Disaster by David A Thomas and Patrick Holmes.
Leo Cooper, London, 1997.
ISBN 0-85052-548-9

WEST, John L
The Loss of 'Lancastria' compiled by John L West.
Millgate, Rossendale, Lancashire, 1988.
ISBN 1-870788-04-4

LIFE IN THE MERCHANT NAVY

BENNETT, GH
Survivors: British Merchant Seamen in the Second World War by GH and
R Bennett.
Hambledon Press, London, 1999.
ISBN 1-85285-182-1

LANE, Tony
The Merchant Seamen's War by Tony Lane.
Manchester University Press, Manchester, 1990.
ISBN 0-7190-2397-1

THOMAS, Gabe
*Milag: Captives of the Kriegsmarine: Merchant Navy Prisoners of War Germany
1939-1945* by Gabe Thomas.
Milag Prisoner of War Association, [Pontardawe, West Glamorgan], 1995.
ISBN 0-9525498-08

RESEARCH FACILITIES AT THE IMPERIAL WAR MUSEUM

THE READING ROOM

Formerly the chapel of the Bethlem Royal Hospital, or Bedlam, this historic room is used extensively by authors, scholars, journalists, broadcasters and visitors alike. Readers have access to a major reference library of printed materials encompassing everything from trench maps to a vast journals collection. The Department of Documents holds an extensive collection of unpublished diaries, letters and memoirs of servicemen and women and civilians.

Access to the Reading Room is free but you should make an appointment in advance.

Monday – Saturday 10.00am-5.00pm
Closed: Bank Holiday weekends, 24, 25, 26 December and for a period of 2 weeks (usually May) for stocktaking purposes

When making an appointment please give us as much detail of your area of research as possible. Material can then be pre-selected and ready on your arrival. However, this should not deter you from a further catalogue search of your own. We will be happy to show you the various catalogues and options open to you. Bags are not generally allowed in the reading room – these should be left in the cloakroom – although handbags and portable computers are admissible. Please remember that this is an old building and, although we have done much to improve the provision of electric points, lighting and ventilation, we are limited by the amount of physical space actually available. We will, however, always try to accommodate anyone wishing to consult our collections. The design limitations of this building make access to the Reading Room difficult for many disabled visitors but alternative facilities are available. Please ask when making your appointment.

Photocopying and other services

Guidance on photocopying procedures is available in printed form in the Reading Room itself. We are bound by the copyright law, and by our own conservation and preservation requirements. Black and white photocopies are available at a fixed Museum price and special photography can be arranged. Booklists and information sheets are available on a variety of subjects.

Our contact details:

Department of Printed Books
Imperial War Museum, Lambeth Road, London SE1 6HZ
Tel: 020 7416 5342 (for general enquiries and appointments)
Fax: 020 7416 5246
Email: books@iwm.org.uk

Department of Documents
Imperial War Museum, Lambeth Road, London SE1 6HZ
Tel: 020 7416 5222
Fax: 020 7416 5374
Email: docs@iwm.org.uk

Other Collecting Departments
[all postal enquiries should be addressed to the appropriate department at Imperial War Museum, Lambeth Road, London SE1 6HZ]

Department of Art
Material may be seen by prior appointment in the Print Room at the Museum's Lambeth Road branch, Tuesday-Thursday, 10.00am-5.00pm. To arrange a visit, contact the Department's Research and Information Officer.
Tel: 020 7416 5228
Email: art@iwm.org.uk

Department of Exhibits and Firearms
A visitor's room is open by appointment, Monday-Friday, 10.00am-5.00pm.
Tel: 020 7416 5308
Fax: 020 7416 5374
Email: exfire@iwm.org.uk

Film and Photograph Archives

The Film Archive is open by appointment from Monday-Friday, 10.00am-5.00pm. At least 24 hours notice is normally sufficient to research the catalogue, but 5-7 days notice is required to view any film selected. Film viewing and handling fees are charged. The Visitor's Room is located at: All Saints Annexe, Austral Street, London SE11.

Tel: 020 7416 5291 / 5292

Fax: 020 7416 5299

Email: film@iwm.org.uk

The Photograph Archive Visitors' Room at the All Saints Annexe, Austral Street, is open to visitors, by appointment, from Monday-Friday, 10.00am-5.00pm.

Tel: 020 7416 5333 / 5338 [Please allow a minimum of 24 hours notice]

Fax: 020 7416 5355

Email: photos@iwm.org.uk

Sound Archive

The Visitors Room at the All Saints Annexe, Austral Street is open by appointment, Monday to Friday, 10.00am-5.00pm. Visitors may listen to tapes and consult printed and database catalogues; some typescripts available.

Tel: 020 7416 5363

Email: sound@iwm.org.uk

Collections Online

An exciting new development has been the launch of **Collections Online** at **www.iwmcollections.org.uk**
The initial tranche of material was made public in 2002, and catalogues from all the Collecting Departments were made

available in 2004. For the first time you can access the Museum's catalogues online. If you want to browse there are short essays on major historical themes, which lead you to selected highlights from all over the collections, including artworks, documents, exhibits, film, photographs and sound recordings. Currently 160,000 records are available, although it is important to realise that no catalogue is ever totally complete – if you don't find what you are looking for, please contact us and ask.

GENERAL CONTACTS

The Museum has five branches. These are:

Imperial War Museum London
Lambeth Road, London SE1 6HZ
Open daily, 10.00am-6.00pm
Tel: 020 7416 5320 / 5321 (general enquiries)
Fax: 020 7416 5374
Email: mail@iwm.org.uk

Churchill Museum and Cabinet War Rooms
Clive Steps, King Charles Street, London SW1A 2AQ
Open daily
Summer (1 April-30 September) 9.30am-6.00pm
last admission 5.15pm
Winter 10.00am-6.00pm, last admission 5.15pm
Tel: 020 7930 6961
Fax: 020 7839 5897
Email: cwr@iwm.org.uk

HMS *Belfast*
Morgan's Lane, Tooley Street, London SE1 2JH
Open daily
Summer (1 March-31 October) 10.00am-6.00pm,
last admission 5.15pm
Winter 10.00am-5.00pm, last admission 4.15pm
Tel: 020 7940 6300
Fax: 020 7403 0719
Email: hmsbelfast@iwm.org.uk

Imperial War Museum Duxford
Cambridgeshire CB2 4QR
Open daily
Summer (mid March-mid October) 10.00am-6.00pm,
last admission 5.15pm
Winter 10.00am-4.00pm, last admission 3.15pm
Tel: 01223 835000
Fax: 01223 837267
Email: duxford@iwm.org.uk

Imperial War Museum North
The Quays, Trafford Wharf, Trafford Park,
Manchester M17 1TZ
Open daily
Summer (1 March-31 October) 10.00am-6.00pm,
last admission 5.30pm
Winter 10.00am-5.00pm, last admission 4.30pm
Tel: 0161 836 4000
Fax: 0161 836 4012
Email: iwmnorth@iwm.org.uk

All branches are closed 24, 25, 26 December

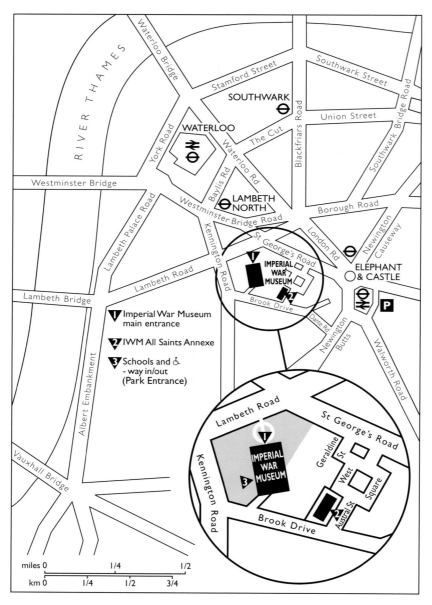

Imperial War Museum main entrance

IWM All Saints Annexe

Schools and ♿ - way in/out (Park Entrance)

www.iwm.org.uk